Rookie
Read-About® Holidays

New Year's Day

By David F. Marx

Consultant
Katharine A. Kane, Reading Specialist
Former Language Arts Coordinator
San Diego County Office of Education

Children's Press®
A Division of Scholastic Inc.
New York   Toronto   London   Auckland   Sydney
Mexico City   New Delhi   Hong Kong
Danbury, Connecticut

Designer: Herman Adler Design Group
Photo Researcher: Caroline Anderson

Library of Congress Cataloging-in-Publication Data

Marx, David F.
    New Year's Day / by David F. Marx.
       p. cm. — (Rookie read-about holidays)
    Includes index.
    ISBN 0-516-22205-8 (lib. bdg.)   0-516-27156-3 (pbk.)
    1. New Year—Juvenile literature. [1. New Year. 2. Holidays.] I. Title.
GT4905.M37   2000
394.2614—dc21

                  00-022636

People celebrate many new things. Some people celebrate the birth of a new baby. Others celebrate moving into a new house.

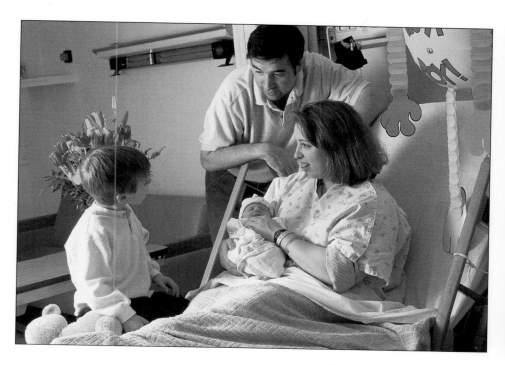

The first day of a new year

On January 1,
we all celebrate
something new . . .
a new year.

Different people have New Year celebrations on different days.

People in India, Korea, and China all have New Year's holidays on days other than January 1.

So do people of the Jewish and Muslim religions.

A New Year's statue from India

A Chinese New Year dance

But just about everyone
in the world celebrates
New Year's Day on
January 1.

January 2006

Sunday	Monday	Tuesday	Wednesday	Thursday	Friday	Saturday
1	2	3	4	5	6	7
8	9	10	11	12	13	14
15	16	17	18	19	20	21
22	23	24	25	26	27	28
29	30	31				

On the calendar that we all share, 2006 becomes 2007, 2007 becomes 2008, and so on.

January 2007

Sunday	Monday	Tuesday	Wednesday	Thursday	Friday	Saturday
	1	2	3	4	5	6
7	8	9	10	11	12	13
14	15	16	17	18	19	20
21	22	23	24	25	26	27
28	29	30	31			

Most New Year celebrations start the night *before* January 1.

December 31 is New Year's Eve.

A New Year's Eve celebration

At 12:00 midnight, December 31 becomes January 1. The new year begins.

People shout "Happy New Year!" and make *lots of noise.*

The new year is here!

New Year's Eve in Times Square

14

Every New Year's Eve, thousands of people celebrate in Times Square in New York City.

They watch a big, lighted ball slowly slide down a pole. It reaches the bottom just as the new year strikes.

The Times Square ball

Many other towns and cities celebrate with "First Night" parties.

Adults and children travel around the town. They listen to concerts and see plays and dance performances.

After people go to bed
on New Year's Eve, the
celebration is not finished.

On New Year's Day, many
towns and cities have parades.

A leopard float made of flowers

The Tournament of Roses Parade takes place in Pasadena, California.

Marching bands and floats wind through the streets.

The beautiful floats are decorated with only roses or other flowers and plants.

Pasadena also hosts the Rose Bowl football game.

The Rose Bowl is one of many big college football games held on or near New Year's Day.

The Rose Bowl football game

Watching football games is just one special way people mark the new year.

Families get together on New Year's Day for a big meal and lots of fun.

When New Year's Day ends, life gets back to normal.

But each year we remember that exciting first moment when we shouted, "Happy New Year!"

Words You Know

birth

Sunday	Monday	Tuesday	Wednesday	Thursday	Friday	Saturday
January 2007						
	1	2	3	4	5	6
7	8	9	10	11	12	13
14	15	16	17	18	19	20
21	22	23	24	25	26	27
28	29	30	31			

calendar

float

January 1

lighted ball

Rose Bowl football game

Times Square

Tournament of Roses
Parade

31

Index

About the Author

David F. Marx is an author and editor of children's books.
He resides in the Chicago area.

Photo Credits